simply romantic®

W9-BLG-785

DATES
on a dime

FamilyLife Publishing®

Little Rock, Arkansas

83391

Dates on a Dime
FamilyLife Publishing®
5800 Ranch Drive
Little Rock, Arkansas 72223
1-800-FL-TODAY • FamilyLife.com
FLTI, d/b/a FamilyLife®, is a ministry of Campus Crusade for Christ, Inc. (known as Cru in the U.S.A.)

ISBN: 978-1-60200-713-0

Cover image: © Stocksy.com/Alie Lengyelova

Printed in the United States of America

2015—Second Edition

21 20 19 18 17   3 4 5 6 7

FAMILYLIFE®

CONTENTS

INTRODUCTION

Try this simple exercise with your spouse tonight: Ask "What is romantic to you?" Listen carefully. Next, share how you describe romance.

We doubt either of you will say "a $500 bottle of perfume," "a new car," or "two-dozen long-stemmed red roses in a crystal vase." Those things are nice, but how many of us can afford them?

The truth is that romance doesn't have to be expensive. It's about thoughtfulness, time together, and the right word at the right time. You simply need forethought and a little creativity.

So if you're short on these, take a look inside. We wrote this book for you. You don't need to try every date, and you may need to adapt them to fit your spouse's idea of romance. Just let these simple suggestions get you started.

Now go ahead, ask the question . . .

FUN 'N' FREE DATES

Enjoy a late night swim with your sweetie
at a nearby lake or pool.

At your local Humane Society,
snuggle and scratch adorable adoptables. Talk
about the pets you had as a child. List their
names, antics, and habits.
TIP: Commit to waiting 24 hours
before deciding to bring a pet home.

On the Fourth of July, grab a blanket and
your sweetheart. Find a secluded spot
to view the local fireworks display.

Cuddle up in the corner of your local library
with an art book or short story that interests
both of you. Choose a color, image,
or word and kiss each time you run across it.

Using your best china, dine by candlelight at
home. Remember to keep it simple:
serve a meal from the grocer's freezer case.

Pack up your portable DVD player or streaming
device. Get out to a quiet spot, then cuddle up
and watch your favorite romantic movie.

Money $aving Tip
Join a babysitting co-op in your
neighborhood or church. For the hours you sit,
you'll earn points to spend on your nights out
for "free" child care. To start a co-op, google
"babysitting co-op" for tips and suggestions.

At Christmastime, pack your car with
a thermos of hot cocoa and two travel
mugs. Drive through local neighborhoods,
sipping your cocoa and viewing the
Christmas light displays. Toast each other
when you've found the most
outrageous display.

Enjoy complimentary concerts at churches
and schools. Check your local newspaper
for a listing of these and other free events.

Appreciation Date!
Take time to verbalize appreciation for each other.
Note his or her inner qualities and physical beauty.

Visit a home improvement store.
Thumb through the books of house
plans and discuss your dream home.

Most museums offer free admission
on certain days. Visit, then bring home
a postcard or trinket from the
gift shop as a memento.

Picnic at the beach or at a
romantic spot nearby. Burn tea lights at
your site, setting them in clear baby-food
jars or other windproof containers.
Don't forget the matches!

Sign up and take a free class at the
local home improvement or garden store.
Then apply your new skills at home.

Money $aving Tip
Search the newspaper, phone book,
or websites for money-saving coupons—
especially for restaurants.

Parades are free—and a lot of fun.
At small-town affairs, you'll enjoy
spotting friends and family in the
band and on the floats. While you may
not spot friends in the big city, the
floats will be larger than life! Big or
little, you can't lose.

Attend a children's sporting event;
they're usually free. Watch closely so
that by the game's end, you can privately
nominate the Most Valuable Player or
Most Enthusiastic Soccer Mom.

Stay in and play a creative version
of your favorite card game.

Find a private location and sunbathe.
Bring coconut-scented oil and apply
liberally to each other.

Money $aving Tip
Empty your pocket change into a jar each
night. Then once a month,
spend your stash on "date night."

Super-Simple Campfire
Bring a bag of ready-to-light charcoal
briquettes and matches to a local campsite or
park. Use it to fuel an evening of
snuggling and cozy chatting.

Check your Sunday paper for a listing of
open houses. As you visit each one,
note your favorite features as idea-starters
for future home improvements.

Go parking in a secluded place.
You have a license for this kind of thing—
for driving and marriage and so forth!

Take the rough out of "roughing it."
For just one evening, camp in your
backyard. Skip the tent so you
can view the stars.

Together, volunteer to do an
elderly person's yard work. Sometimes
reaching out to others can bring you
together like nothing else can.

Test-drive your fantasy car together.

Take time for a quiet stroll together through
moonlit snow or during a light rain.

Body Art
Mix 1 egg yolk, 1/2 tsp. water,
and a drop or two of food coloring.
Paint each other and create
temporary tattoos.

The best time to star gaze is
during the Perseids, which peak August
12 or 13, and the Geminids, which peak
the nights of December 13 or 14.
For more info see
www.amsmeteors.org/meteor-showers

During the spring or summer, pick wildflowers. Gather a bouquet for your nightstand and, if you still remember how, weave a clover or daisy chain for her.

Use sidewalk chalk to declare your love:
When you stroll through town or down a
paved trail, leave a testament of your love
by drawing your initials into a heart with
an arrow through it. As you make your way
home on this same path, stop and kiss at
each marker you've created.

$15 DATES

Cruise the aisles of the dollar store for gifts
for each other. Meet up in the car, where
you can exchange gifts and kisses.

Don't miss a trip to the pumpkin patch this fall. Decorate your front door or hearth with your fun finds.

Shop the grocery store together for a few favorite dessert toppings. Build and share your own special sundae.

Enjoy community theatre at
a fraction of the price of a
Broadway production.

Create your own version of a
kitchen challenge. Seperately purchase
mystery ingredients for your spouse to use
for dinner or dessert preparation.
Taste each other's dishes and
declare a winner.

Pick berries at a u-pick farm.
On the following Saturday morning,
treat yourselves to fresh blueberry
pancakes or strawberry-topped
Belgian waffles.

Monday is often a discount day at
the state or county fair. Share some
cotton candy and a funnel cake!

Many communities have a farmer's market
in the summer and fall. Purchase some
fresh veggies while enjoying the outdoors.

Relive your high school days at the
roller rink. Ask the DJ to play "your" song
for a couples' skate.

Eat cheap at an all-night diner.

With a cup of coffee in hand, visit
the travel section of a bookstore.
Purchase a map or inexpensive travel guide to
take home and plan your dream vacation.

Pretend you are a tourist in your own town.
As you visit fun places, ask passersby to snap
photos of you and your honey. Make sure to
get some photos printed for
romantic memories.

Split an entrée at your favorite local restaurant.

At a local thrift shop, purchase silly
souvenirs commemorating your
time together.

Try your hand at pool. With a fifteen-dollar
budget you might be able to afford a snack.

Money $aving Tip
When eating out, order water as
your beverage of choice—it's usually free.

Purchase the fixings for a gourmet pizza and spend time in the kitchen making it together.

Create a vending machine meal
for two. Extra points if you can score
all four food groups!

Movie matinees are usually less crowded—
which means you can choose a seat in the
back row and steal a few kisses.

Search out local attractions that
you may not already know about:
planetariums, arboretums, walking trails,
etc. Have fun discovering together.

Treat yourselves to an ice cream sundae.
Consider sharing one.

Money $aving Tip
Invest in your marriage by planning a
monthly date night and including the
cost in your budget.

Many restaurant portions are huge! Skip
the entrée and go for appetizers and drinks.

Spend time together at a coffee house.
You can find lots of coffee-date ideas in the
book *Coffee Dates for Couples*.

State and national parks are affordable.
Pack a lunch and enjoy the great outdoors.

Most cities and many neighborhoods
offer inexpensive and fun festivals. Google
"festival" and your city's name for ideas
and schedules.

Money $aving Tip
Consider double- or triple-dating
where group rates apply. You can
save money and double your fun!

Compete with each other at the driving
range or miniature golf course. Loser buys
the post-game refreshments.

Google "drive-in theater" or "movies in
the park." Box up some dinner, snacks,
and a blanket and head over. Snuggle up
with your honey and enjoy the show.

$25 DATES

When the carnival comes to town,
make some memories. Ride the rides, buy
some snacks, and try your hand
at the games.

Feel daring? Shop for a new
piece of lingerie together—something
you both like. Ladies, model it
that evening.

Consider an easy, lazy, weekend brunch—
lots of food at a reasonable price.

Go go-carting! First one in the pit
gets the ice cream flavor of choice
at a "pit stop" on the way home.

Money $aving Tip
You'll find that most events are
cheaper in the daytime. Head to a matinee
to see a play, order off the lunch menu, or
get the "twilight rate" at the movies.

After a holiday party or special event,
since you're all dressed up, head to a
swanky restaurant to share dessert.

Plan a fast-food progressive dinner. Share an appetizer at one eatery, an entrée at another, and finish by splitting dessert elsewhere.

Check online for a
"paint your own pottery" studio.
Spend time creating a memorable
piece for your collection.

Rent a paddleboat at a nearby lake.
Don't forget to pack a picnic lunch or dinner.

Find a restaurant that serves high tea.
Pretend you are the rulers of your own kingdom.
How would you treat your subjects?

Order Chinese takeout
and dine in a fun and interesting place.
Write your own fortunes for each other.

Use Friday morning's paper to map the
local garage sales. Then on Saturday morning,
shop with a budget of twenty-five dollars.
Purchase something special for your home.

Purchase two tickets to a minor league baseball or arena football game. Take your own peanuts.

Plan an anniversary surprise for
your close friends! Sneak out late that night
and place an anniversary card with a $25
gift card to their favorite restaurant on
their front door or car windshield.

Scout out a driving, biking, or walking
tour in or near your city. Learn something new
together. Stop and grab a dessert or
beverage along the way.

Enjoy drama or sporting events
on a local high school campus.

INEXPENSIVE GETAWAYS

Grab or borrow camping gear and
head for the hills. Spend the weekend
enjoying the outdoors and each other.

Take advantage of the weekend
specials that most hotels offer. Get a room
with a hot tub and BYOBB (bring your
own bubble bath).

Money $aving Tip
Find ways to collect points that can be
redeemed for free flights and hotel rooms.
Then cash them in on a trip for the
two of you—alone.

House-sit for friends or family
while they are out of town. Make it a
special getaway without leaving town.

If you or your spouse travel for business,
take the trip together. You'll save on
lodging expenses—and transportation if
you drive instead of fly.

Rent a cabin in the off-season. Take along groceries to save on the cost of eating out.

Send the kids to Grandma's house
for the weekend. Turn your home into
"Fantasy Island."

Money $aving Tip
Check out your employee benefits
packages. They might include special
rates on theme parks, hotels, etc.

Check with your local travel agent
or search online for a quaint
Bed & Breakfast Inn.

Ask friends and church members
if any own a vacation or weekend home.
Arrange to rent or borrow it
for the weekend.

Take a trip down memory lane.
Arrange to spend a few days in your
childhood hometown.

Plan a mini-vacation with another couple—
sharing the expense of lodging and the
work of cooking and cleaning up.

Steal away to a bed and breakfast during the week.
The rates are lower than those on weekends.

Some monasteries and convents open their
doors to guests for little or no charge.
Spend time praying for your marriage.

MY CHEAP DATE IDEAS

MY CHEAP DATE IDEAS

_____

_____

_____

_____

_____

_____

_____

_____

_____

FAMILYLIFE® presents

weekend to remember®

GREAT MARRIAGES DON'T JUST *happen.*

Great marriages require intentionality and investment—just like a garden that must be watered in order to grow.

FamilyLife's Weekend to Remember is a two-and-a half day weekend getaway that offers:

- biblically-based insights from top speakers and marriage experts;
- relaxing time alone together, free from distractions; and
- helpful tools and resources for an immediate impact on your marriage.

Get intentional about taking your marriage to the next level.

SAVE $100
per couple.

Go to
WeekendtoRemember.com
or call
1-800-FL-TODAY
and use group code
FLPFRIENDS.

FAN THE FLAMES OF ROMANCE!

Tips to Romance Your Husband and *Tips to Romance Your Wife* bring spark and sizzle to your marriage. Learn to communicate heart to heart, express love through food and fun, give gifts that say, "I love you!" and romance your love on birthdays and holidays. Heat up your marriage with these creative ideas and become *Simply Romantic!*

Shop.FamilyLife.com • 1-800-FL-TODAY